A BOOK OF SHIVERY POEMS
Catch Your Breath

Selected by Lilian Moore and Lawrence Webster

Illustrated by Gahan Wilson

GARRARD PUBLISHING COMPANY
CHAMPAIGN, ILLINOIS

Library of Congress Cataloging in Publication Data
Moore, Lilian, comp.
  Catch your breath.
  (Reading shelf series)
  SUMMARY: Poems about unusual or frightening things.
Includes as topics Halloween, witches, and creepy
creatures.
  1. Children's poetry. [1. Poetry — Collections.
2. Superstition — Poetry] I. Webster, Lawrence,
1947-   joint comp. II. Wilson, Gahan, illus.
III. Title.
PZ8.3.M7835 Cat   821'.008'03   72-11759
ISBN 0-8116-4113-9

The editors and publisher acknowledge with thanks permission received to reprint the poems in this collection.

Acknowledgments and formal notices of copyright for all
material under copyright appear on pages 62 and 63, which are
hereby made an extension of the copyright page.

Contents

All Kinds of Shivers

There's a long funny shiver
that feels like an "ooooh!"
when things queer and eerie
spring out and say "boo!"

There's the quick little shiver
you suddenly feel
when things that are scary
are a little bit real.

There's a dee-licious shiver
that comes with a wiggle
for an odd spooky joke
that ends in a giggle.

There are those creatures
and all of their kin,
whose ways are so creepy
they tingle the skin.

And then there's the shivery
moment of change
when the everyday world
looks suddenly strange.

L. M.

The Pumpkin

You may not believe it,
for hardly could I:
I was cutting a pumpkin
to put in a pie,
And on it was written
in letters most plain
"You may hack me in slices,
but I'll grow again."

I seized it and sliced it
and made no mistake
As, with dough rounded over,
I put it to bake:
But soon in the garden
as I chanced to walk,
Why, there was that pumpkin
entire on his stalk!

Robert Graves

Footprints in the Night

Who came to our door
in the dead of the night
while the foghorns groaned
and the long eaves wept?

Whoever came
neither rapped nor called,
not the smallest sound
reached where we slept.

Whoever came
to the cold doorstone
paused and listened
and then went on.

Small steps in the snow
show whence he came,
and small steps point
the way he has gone.

Elizabeth Coatsworth

Alas, Alack!

Ann, Ann!
    Come! quick as you can!
There's a fish that *talks*
    In the frying pan.
Out of the fat,
    As clear as glass,
He put up his mouth
    And moaned "Alas!"
Oh most mournful,
    "Alas, alack!"
Then turned to his sizzling
    And sank him back.

Walter de la Mare

Queer

I seem to see
in the apple tree,
I seem to know
from the field below,
I seem to hear
when the woods are near,
I seem to sense
by the farmer's fence,
I seem to place
just the faintest trace,
I seem to smell
what I can't quite tell,
I seem to feel
that it isn't real,
I seem to guess
at it, more or less.

David McCord

Mean Song

Snickles and podes,
Ribble and grodes:
That's what I wish you.

A nox in the groot,
A root in the stoot
And a gock in the forbeshaw, too.

Keep out of sight
For fear that I might
Glom you a gravely snave.

Don't show your face
Around any place
Or you'll get
one flack snack in the bave.

Eve Merriam

No One Heard Him Call

He went down to the woodshed
To put his bike away.
There was no moon.
There were no stars.
He ran the whole dark way.
And when he hurried back again
The porch light had gone out!
He couldn't find the doorknob,
So then he gave a shout.

It wasn't very loud, though,
And no one heard him call.
He pounded with his knuckles;
Still no one came at all.
But then where he was standing
A *light* came streaming wide:
"My goodness, is that you?"
she said.
And he was safe inside!

Dorothy Aldis

Curtain World

When I am almost awake in the morning,
The room is in half light.
I look up at my long red curtains
And see faces of people,
Scary people,
And dragons and monsters.
I am in the curtain world
Where nothing is the same.

Heather Morse

When I Was Lost

Underneath my belt
My stomach was a stone.
Sinking was the way I felt.
And hollow.
And alone.

Dorothy Aldis

Night Storm

I wake
when lightning cracks
its silver whip
and starts wild lions
running roaring
overhead
and great white thunder-horses
galloping
around my bed.

I hide
under the covers till they ride
away.

Jane Sherman

As I Was Going Out One Day

As I was going out one day
My head fell off and rolled away.
But when I saw that it was gone,
I picked it up and put it on.

And when I got into the street
A fellow cried: "Look at your feet!"
I looked at them and sadly said:
"I've left them both asleep in bed!"

Anonymous

Beware, My Child

Beware, my child,
of the snaggle-toothed beast.
He sleeps till noon,
then makes his feast
on Hershey bars
and cakes of yeast
and anyone around—o.

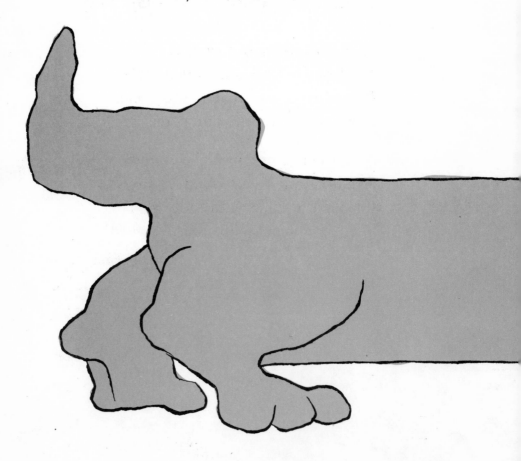

So when you see him,
sneeze three times
and say three loud
and senseless rhymes
and give him all your
saved-up dimes,
or else you'll ne'er be found—o.

Shel Silverstein

Lancaster County Tragedy

Pennsylvania Dutch Mouse
Is mourned by all his kin.
He should have gone the door out
But he went the house cat in.

                    W. Lowrie Kay

Algy

Algy saw a bear;
The bear saw Algy.
The bear had a bulge;
The bulge was Algy.

                    Folk Rhyme

From . . .

How to Tell the Wild Animals

If strolling forth, a beast you view,
    Whose hide with spots is peppered,
As soon as he has lept on you,
    You'll know it is the Leopard.
'Twill do no good to roar with pain,
He'll only lep and lep again.

Carolyn Wells

From . . .

We Must Be Polite

(Lessons for children on how to
behave under peculiar circumstances)

If we meet a gorilla
what shall we do?
Two things we may do
if we so wish to do.

Speak to the gorilla,
very, very respectfully,
"How do you do, sir?"

Or speak to him with less
distinction of manner,
"Hey, why don't you go back
where you came from?"

Carl Sandburg

What Someone Told Me
About Bobby Link

What do you think
Of Bobby Link?
He went for a swim
with nothing to drink
But iced tea, hot tea,
Milk in a jug,
Cherry pop, coffee,
Beer in a mug,
And a hat full of rain,
And a cup full of snow.
He was never seen again,
And some who know
Say he got so wet
When he drank it all down
That he isn't dry yet.
—I hope he didn't drown.

John Ciardi

Ezra Shank

He rocked the boat
Did Ezra Shank.
These bubbles mark

o

o

o

Where Ezra sank.

Whiz Bang

The Worm

When the earth is turned in spring
The worms are fat as anything.

And birds come flying all around
To eat the worms right off the ground.

They like worms just as much as I
Like bread and milk and apple pie.

And once, when I was very young,
I put a worm right on my tongue.

I didn't like the taste a bit,
And so I didn't swallow it.

But oh, it makes my mother squirm
Because she *thinks* I ate that worm!

Ralph Bergengren

A Witch Story

From ...

The Witch in the Wintry Wood

This is the tale of how Tim one
night
didn't start home until
candlelight
when the sky was black and the
snow was white.
Woo-HOO, woo-HOO, woo-HOO.

He walked through the woods
like a frightened goat,
his muffler twisted around his
throat,
expecting to jump at a witch's
note:
"Woo-HOO, woo-HOO, woo-HOO."

Out of the night came a sheep
dog's yowl,
which Tim was sure was a
witch's howl,
a terrible witch on a wintry
prowl.
Woo-HOO, woo-HOO, woo-HOO.

Tim, the timid, began to
race,
certain he sighted a witch's face
back of each shadowy hiding
place.
Woo-HOO, woo-HOO, woo-HOO.

He ran through the woods on his
lonely trek
till horrors! a hand went around
his neck,
holding his headlong flight in
check.
Woo-HOO, woo-HOO, woo-HOO.

Nobody knows how long he
stood
with that hand on his throat in
the silent wood
until he could find some
hardihood . . .
Woo-HOO, woo-HOO, woo-HOO.

Then he looked around like a
shaky calf,
thinking of words for his
epitaph,
and "Oh, ho, ho!" he began
to laugh . . .
Woo-HOO, woo-HOO, woo-HOO.

For what he saw was a funny
sight—
it wasn't a witch at his throat
by night,
but a pine branch pulling his
muffler tight!
Woo-HOO, woo-HOO, woo-HOO.

Aileen Fisher

The Shivers of Halloween

Witch?

On a dark
and lonely street
I met a witch
complete
with broom and switch
and pointed hat
and cat.

So
I turned,
fled
sped on trembling feet.
Now I'll never know.
Did I really meet
a witch,
or someone playing
Trick or Treat?

Sam Reavin

A Cat's Life

Cats prowl late at night
    And spend mornings basking.
They visit the neighbors
    Without ever asking.

Cats climb over fences
    And leap over ditches,
And ride on long broomsticks
    With Halloween witches!

Eleanor Struthers

How Come?

They say it's just a pumpkin,
Just a big old pumpkin
That was growing on a vine;
And to make a Jack-o'-lantern,
A big old Jack-o'-lantern
They thought a big old pumpkin
would be fine.

So they made a Jack-o'-lantern,
A grinning Jack-o'-lantern,
And they put a light inside
for all to see.
But if it's just a pumpkin,
Just a big old pumpkin,
How come that Jack-o'-lantern
winked at me?

                              Sara Asheron

Mr. Macklin's Jack-o'-Lantern

Mr. Macklin takes his knife
And carves the yellow pumpkin face:
Three holes bring eyes and nose to life,
The mouth has thirteen teeth in place.

Then Mr. Macklin just for fun
Transfers the corn-cob pipe from his
Wry mouth to Jack's, and everyone
Dies laughing! O what fun it is

Till Mr. Macklin draws the shade
And lights the candle in Jack's skull.
Then all the inside dark is made
As spooky and as horrorful

As Halloween, and creepy crawl
The shadows on the tool-house floor,
With Jack's face dancing on the wall.
O Mr. Macklin! Where's the door?

David McCord

Shivers

Bushes quiver
where shadows lean,
and not a sliver
of moon is seen.

Near the river
some goblins (green)
with a witch in front
and a ghost between

Make me sh . . i . . vvvver,
but I am keen
about the shivers
of Halloween.

Aileen Fisher

The Silent Snake

The birds go fluttering in the air,
    The rabbits run and skip,
Brown squirrels race along the bough,
    The May-flies rise and dip;
But while these creatures play and leap,
The silent snake goes *creepy-creep!*

The birdies sing and whistle loud,
　　The busy insects hum,
The squirrels chat, the frogs say "Crook!"
　　But the snake is always dumb.
With not a sound through grasses deep
The silent snake goes *creepy-creep!*

Anonymous

About the Teeth of Sharks

The thing about a shark is—teeth,
One row above, one row beneath.

Now take a close look. Do you find
It has another row behind?

Still closer—here, I'll hold your hat:
Has it a third row behind that?

Now look in and . . . Look out! Oh my,
I'll *never* know now! Well, good-bye.

John Ciardi

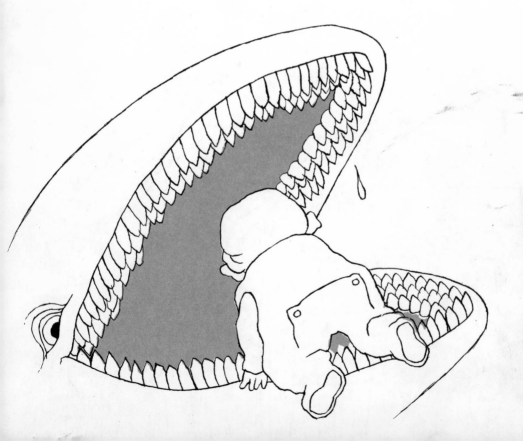

Moon

I have a white cat whose name is Moon;
He eats catfish from a wooden spoon,
And sleeps till five each afternoon.

Moon goes out when the moon is bright
And sycamore trees are spotted white
To sit and stare in the dead of night.

Beyond still water cries a loon,
Through mulberry leaves peers a wild baboon
And in Moon's eyes I see the moon.

William Jay Smith

Boa Constrictor

Oh I'm being eaten by a boa constrictor,
A boa constrictor, a boa constrictor,
I'm being eaten by a boa constrictor,
And I don't like it . . . one bit!
Well what do you know . . .
it's nibbling my toe,
Oh gee . . . it's up to my knee,
Oh my . . . it's up to my thigh,
Oh fiddle . . . it's up to my middle,
Oh heck . . . it's up to my neck,
Oh dread . . . it's . . . MMFFF.

Shel Silverstein

Snake

Very thin
and opaque
is the skin
of a snake.

Let it shed,
let it wane
to this dead
cellophane.

Let it be:
I've no itch
to see
which is which.

David McCord

Octopus

Take this solemn tip
from us.
Never once forget it.
Do not hug an
octopus
or you'll regret it.

It can be said
he has a head,
but the most-li-est of him
is eight
long
strong
and snaky arms.
There isn't
any
rest of him.

Sam Reavin

If you should meet a crocodile,
    Don't take a stick and poke him;
Ignore the welcome in his smile,
    Be careful not to stroke him.
For as he sleeps upon the Nile,
    He thinner gets and thinner;
And whene'er you meet a crocodile
    'He's ready for his dinner.

Author Unknown

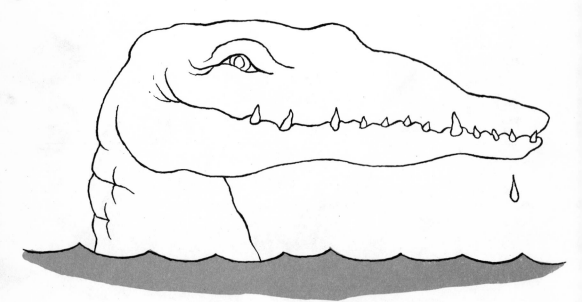

Supper for a Lion

Savage lion in the zoo,
Walking by on padded feet,
To and fro and fro and to,
You seem to think it's time to eat.

Then how about a bowl of stew
With jello for dessert? Or would
A juicy bone be best for you?

Oh, please don't stare
as though you knew
That I'd taste good!

Dorothy Aldis

Suddenly Strange

I saw the wind to-day:
I saw it in the pane
Of glass upon the wall:
A moving thing,—'twas like
No bird with widening wing,
No mouse that runs along
The meal bag under the beam.

I think it like a horse,
All black, with frightening mane,
That springs out of the earth,
And tramples on his way.
I saw it in the glass,
The shaking of a mane:
A horse that no one rides!

Padraic Colum

The Wind

The wind stood up, and gave a shout;
He whistled on his fingers, and

Kicked the withered leaves about
And thumped the branches with his hand,

And he said he'll kill, and kill, and kill;
And so he will; And so he will!

James Stephens

The Wind and the Moon

Said the Wind to the Moon,
"I will blow you out;
    You stare
    In the air
    Like a ghost in a chair
Always looking what I am about.
I hate to be watched—
I'll blow you out."

George MacDonald

Sea Calm

How still,
How strangely still
The water is today.
It is not good
For water
To be so still that way.

Langston Hughes

Martian

Is it a Martian creature
    coming to crush me?
        I close my eyes and then
            open them to see

the branching antenna
    of a TV.

Eve Merriam

Someone

Someone
is climbing
the wall
of the farmer's house.
How slow he is,
how still.
Now
his head
is close,
close to the sill.
In a moment
he will
enter the room.
Yet
no one has given a
squeal
of alarm.
For what can the shadow
of a scarecrow
steal?

Sam Reavin

Mag

Mag! Mag! Stuff a rag
Under the window.
The wind's a hag
Creeping nearer, near, nearer,
Calling clearer, clearer, clearer,
Grab a rag, grab a paper!
Mag!

Patricia Hubbell

Winter Evening

One evening, coming home when I should,
I climbed the backyard fence and stood
Outside my house and watched night grow
Darker—till softly down came snow.

The flakes fell silently until
The ground and grass were white and still,
And only a little way away
Bushes seemed far and tall and grey

As trees in a wood where bears could hide!
And so I quietly went inside.

Harry Behn

Echo

Hello!

    hello!

Are you near?

    near, near.

Or far from here?

    far, far from here.

Are you there?

    there, there

Or coming this way,
Haunting my words
Whatever I say?

Halloo!

    halloooo

Listen, you.
Who are you, anyway?

    who, who, whoooo?

Sara Asheron

Acknowledgments

Atheneum Publishers, Inc.: For "Mean Song" by Eve Merriam. Copyright © 1962 by Eve Merriam. From *There Is No Rhyme for Silver*. Used by permission of Atheneum Publishers. For "Mag" by Patricia Hubbell. Copyright © 1968 by Patricia Hubbell. From *Catch Me a Wind*. Used by permission of Atheneum Publishers.

Atlantic-Little, Brown and Co.: For "The Worm" by Ralph Bergengren from *Jane, Joseph and John* by Ralph Bergengren. For "Moon" by William Jay Smith from *Laughing Time*. Copyright 1955 by William Jay Smith. By permission of Atlantic-Little, Brown and Co.

The Atlantic Monthly Company: For "Lancaster County Tragedy" by W. Lowrie Kay. Copyright © 1967 by the Atlantic Monthly Company, Boston, Massachusetts. Reprinted with permission.

Sara Asheron: For "Echo" and "How Come?" Reprinted by permission of the author who controls all rights. Copyright © by Sara Asheron.

Collins-Knowlton-Wing, Inc.: For "The Pumpkin" by Robert Graves. Reprinted by permission of Collins-Knowlton-Wing, Inc. Copyright ©. All rights reserved.

Padraic Colum: For "I Saw the Wind Today." Reprinted by permission.

Dodd, Mead & Company, Inc.: For "How to Tell the Wild Animals" by Carolyn Wells. Reprinted by permission of Dodd, Mead & Company, Inc., from *Baubles* by Carolyn Wells. Copyright 1917 by Dodd, Mead & Company, Inc. Copyright renewed 1945.

Aileen Fisher: For "The Witch in the Wintry Wood" and "Shivers" by permission of the author, Aileen Fisher.

Harcourt Brace Jovanovich, Inc.: For "We Must Be Polite" by Carl Sandburg. Copyright © 1950 by Carl Sandburg. Reprinted from his volume, *Wind Song*, by permission of Harcourt Brace Jovanovich, Inc. For "Winter Evening" by Harry Behn from *The Wizard in the Well*. Copyright © 1956 by Harry Behn. Reprinted by permission of Harcourt Brace Jovanovich, Inc.

Index of Authors